A PRINCIPAL SPEAKS:

Observations; Experiences;
Opinions; Recommendations;
Conclusions

* Dear Nell,
        I've enjoyed every
minute of interacting with
you and hope that it can
continue in the future.
        Thank you for recommending
Carmen to me — She is super.
        Be well and stay in touch

Johns

-HODN

A PRINCIPAL SPEAKS:

Observations; Experiences;
Opinions; Recommendations;
Conclusions

John Hodnett, Jr.

To order additional copies of this book, contact:
Xlibris Corporation
1-888-795-4274
www.Xlibris.com
Orders@Xlibris.com

CONTENTS

PREFACE

One of the most discussed topics in the country is education. We approach it from all angles and go into great depths describing positive and negative points about what is being done, changes that need to be made, what the cost will be and where we should get the money to pay for the changes. There seems to be no limit to the number of proposals for meeting the needs of our ailing system of educating our children.

These discussions might take place in any area where at least a few people congregate and might include audiences of thousands at conferences or meetings and on TV. People who do most of the talking are in positions ranging from the top federal and state positions to the parent. It appears to be popular in federal, state and local campaigns. The one group which seems to do the least talking is the one which should have the most to say — the principals, including their support group of administrators and supervisors. Without their input, the information going out to the public is likely to be less than the full story.

As a principal of fifteen years, I shudder when I hear some of the proposals or listen to some of the thoughts coming out of these discussions. My 31+ years of total experience in education, plus three years as an officer in the U. S. Navy, taught me to be and do things slightly different than what I see and hear coming from these discussions. The following pages contain condensed versions of some of the ideas, thoughts, perceptions, recommendations, conclusions, etc. that are the results of my experiences, involvement, observations and my positive relationships with past colleagues, staff and children. There are no footnotes or reference lists. My memory has been my compass and I hope that it did not deviate from its charted course.

INTRODUCTION

My conscious life and learning began when I was about three years old. The first thing I remember is that I had been playing in the yard on a Sunday afternoon, had gotten sick and was trying to keep my favorite red short pants from getting dirty. This was a special occasion because I did not get to wear these pants every day. I can not remember what the special occasion was, but I do know that it was a beautiful, warm day since the sun was shining and I was wearing only a white shirt with short sleeves with the pants.

Since my father was a sharecropper, this incident took place on a tobacco farm which was loaded with opportunities for learning. One had to learn how to do most jobs in order to have a smooth operation. Learning for survival required knowing construction and maintenance of adequate shelter; food getting, storage and preparation; the operation and maintenance of all machinery; and recognition of illnesses and how to deal with them. Improvisation was required on a daily basis in schedules, procedures, maintenance and operational procedures. Nature, animals and plants had to be recognized, understood, used and conserved in order to keep things in balance. As a general rule, one either learned well or he was not a successful farmer.

Children had to begin to learn early in life and become competent in doing tasks, some of which were normally done by older siblings or adults. A pocket knife was a standard item almost every boy owned, carried and knew how to use responsibly. The use of other tools was mastered as one became larger and strong enough to manipulate them. Many boys and fathers used these tools to make the only toys that were present in their homes with which children would play.

While sharecropping does not rank very high on the list of preferred occupations, it happens to be one of the best for an inquisitive mind. Not only can it be a learning lab in which you can experiment and from which you can learn, but it also is an almost perfect setting for applying or trying ideas you learn in school or other places.

My major area of study in college was determined partly by things I had learned and become interested in on the farm. On a practical basis, I had learned quite a bit in the areas of Botany, Zoology, Earth Science, Horticulture, Genetics, Engineering, Agriculture, Physics, and some other related areas. I did not choose my area of study because I wanted to return to the farm, but rather because it was an area I had some knowledge of and liked.

I hope I have not given the impression that I have been selling or "putting down" sharecropping or farming. My purpose has been to point out that learning takes place in almost any setting. You do not need special equipment, you learn by doing and applying learned concepts to daily living experiences in order for it to be meaningful and you succeed better in areas of study that you like. Any occupation, setting, equipment, or materials may be used to provide a basis for a positive learning experience.

CHAPTER I

Who is Being Taught?

A casual observation of any class might give you the idea that it is a fairly homogeneous mixture of children who are basically the same age and size. You might also get the idea that they have basically the same habits, abilities, attention spans, self-concepts, interests and other characteristics in common. A closer study will reveal that hardly any of this is true.

As chairman of a junior high school science department, I was asked to choose a high performing group of children, set up a special class, develop a curriculum and teach the children on a level that would qualify them for entry as a unit into the honors program of the high school. I spared no effort in attempting to complete the task as requested.

In developing this program, every desirable procedure,

technique, standard and material available was used. I requested recommendations from teachers and counselors and obtained permission from parents. The staff checked classroom achievement levels and evaluated learning styles. We obtained and studied IQ levels, standardized reading and math scores and personality characteristics. We interviewed each child to determine his or her maturity and interest in such a program. The end result was a group of 30+ children who appeared almost identical on paper: 140+ IQ; reading scores at least 2 years above grade level; math scores at least 2 years above grade level; personable and mature enough to assume a high level of responsibility. The perfect class!

After working with the class for a few weeks, my initial excitement began to decrease as problems common to so-called "regular" classes began to emerge. I was beginning to see that, except for the higher level of thinking ability, I was faced with the same problems of a "regular" class, as well as the same basic differences among children and learning styles as in any other class, although the children interacted at a more rapid and intense pace. Furthermore, in testing, I discovered that the graph of performance levels of the students produced the well-known bell-shaped curve usually obtained by graphing the performance levels of a randomly grouped class. Needless to say, I discovered that I was not teaching the "perfect" class.

This experience, plus experience with other classes, provided evidence that all children are individuals with unique characteristics. Ability level, performance level, and personality traits do not change that fact. The following few pages give some examples of the types of children who make up the classes in our schools.

Jerry was always present, seated at his desk in the rear of the room. He was always prepared for class and displayed commendable behavior. He did not volunteer to participate but generally responded correctly if questioned and also participated in class experiments or activities if requested to do so. He was not an enthusiastic performer but had a numerical grade average of above 95. He usually brought with him math materials, and when his full attention was not required, he was generally working on some math problems of his own. We didn't know his exact IQ, but it was above 180. We did know that his primary interest was in math and that he needed to be in a class that would permit him to explore and expand his capabilities. Working with his parents, we were able to get him into a special university math class that met on Saturdays. Toward the end of his 9th grade year, he appeared on TV giving explanations for some of his original math derivations.

Chris had an IQ of 145. He had an electronics library in his home that any professional would envy, and he loved to experiment and work in this field. He was bored in the regular classroom studying general science because he already knew all of the material. So, with permission of the school administration, we made a deal that was mutually beneficial. I would permit him to spend his science period in my AV room repairing AV equipment as long as he did all required experiments and took all tests. Chris was the first and only student I taught who made perfect scores on every test for the whole year. He completed 9th grade at the age of 13 and entered MIT at 16.

Jim was a most unusual boy. He was always happy and smiling no matter what happened. Apparently he could not be embarrassed or insulted. He was anxious to please and would do anything anyone requested. His academic skills were not on a high level but it did not seem to bother him that he was not doing work on the same level as the rest of the class. He was happy with himself as a person and his performance. He sucked his fingers — all four at a time — and seemed to get a kick out of it when other boys complained that he was getting spit all over everything and asked for seats away from him. In spite of all of these characteristics, other students liked him and were even protective of him, although they sometimes appeared as if they wanted to kill him.

Bonnie was an unusually physically mature and beautiful girl for age 15 and was acutely aware of her charm. She used every skill she possessed to get all desirable males (including teachers) to like her as much as she liked herself. Academics were not her interest and she did only what she had to do. She could be influenced by a male teacher if he happened to be her idol and if he didn't approach her in a threatening manner. Even then, her idol had to be extra strong and consistent in his demands and requirements of her. Underneath the flashy exterior, Bonnie was still a kid at heart and reacted as such if you could reach her.

According to IQ and achievement tests, many students rank very high but do not measure up in their daily academic performance. Helen earned the highest achievement test score in her grade at the end of the school year. For the next year, she was placed in a class and with a teacher who supposedly would provide the structure and environment for her to advance according to her ability. It did not take long, however, to discover that she could not perform effectively in this setting because she lacked personal initiative.

HODN

She needed a change of class and type of teacher to get her to use her innate ability.

William was in a special progress class designed to complete three years' work in two. Naturally, all of the students were advanced in all areas of measured abilities. Performance levels were higher than for regular classes — the passing grade was 85. But, William consistently fell a bit short on tests and laboratory work results. He sometimes complained that he could not see from where he was sitting, so we moved him to the front of the room. This helped somewhat but did not completely solve the problem. At the end of the year, when William did not have the required average to attend the special high school his parents strongly wanted him to enter, they came in to discuss the reason. It turned out that William had very poor vision which his glasses did not completely correct. The parents had been aware of the problem but had not let the school know because they were afraid that if the special school was aware of the problem, it would keep him from gaining admission. Unfortunately, it was the parents in this case who kept William from going to the special school and caused him to be removed from the special track.

Peter came from a middle class single-parent home. He was a first grade student who was severely anxious about going to school. In fact, he had been taken to a doctor and given

Ritalin each morning before school so that he would be manageable. Peter was referred to the principal who accepted the child and the problem. The principal saw him each morning and took him on a walk around the campus while counseling and developing a positive relationship with him. It didn't take too long before Peter began to like coming to the office and going to his classroom. Soon he no longer needed the Ritalin and became a very happy first grader.

Children from homeless and migrant worker families present a unique set of problems that present challenges for school systems. Some of the more prominent ones include:

1. No records showing proper grade placement, last school attended, performance level, health information, etc.
2. Low attendance,
3. Little or no parental involvement,
4. Improper physical care and poor nutrition,
5. Low self-esteem, and
6. Low interest level.

The existence of these problems does not mean that these children cannot be taught. What it does mean is that in order for them to be taught effectively, these problems must be addressed and overcome through special means and educational resources that adapt to the composition of the group.

Because of changes in the structure and employment demands on families, it has become necessary for some children to go home to empty houses in the afternoon and lock themselves in until their parents come home from work. This is particularly critical for children who live in high crime areas. They are deprived of normal outside play, socialization and recreation with other children. This condition has its effect on both physical and emotional development. In addition, when left alone for any length of time, most children will conjure up activities that can be unsafe, bad for them and even injurious or fatal. In order to prevent such unwholesome activities, some schools and/or teachers who normally work late, provide after-school supervision.

Extended day schools operate on a schedule generally covering the daily period of 7:00 am to 6:00 pm or some variation of that. The basic idea is to provide instruction and supervision of children so that their parents can get to work on time and spend the normal work day on the job without worrying about their child(ren). This program is particularly helpful to single parent families. This day is extremely long for K-5 children and the effect is seen in many ways with many of the children. Some come in sleepy, without breakfast, lack of personal attention, lack of emotional attention and homework not done. These children generally need some special attention and parents need to be made aware of such along with any special help needed.

Occasionally, we have a pleasant surprise in having an overachiever. I am thinking of Jane, who was the top student in her class in all subject areas. Because her record indicated that she had an IQ of 74, teachers initially disbelieved that she was capable of such high performance and requested to have her tested again. (In fact, she was re-tested twice with basically the same results.) There remained some non-believers, but she demonstrated that she did possess the ability and motivation, completing the year as the top student in her class and on her grade level.

Parents don't generally like for their children to be bused, and children don't like it either, except for the occasional excitement en route. But enthusiasm palls as some of the trips last for an hour or more. As they leave the bus in the morning their body language, attitude and conversation give clues as to how they feel about being bused. Many are exhausted from having to get up so early and from such a long ride. Some find the trip physically and emotionally disturbing. Others openly express feelings about the driver or unpleasant events that occur during a trip. Many other reactions and attitudes arise from:

1. Knowledge of the unfairness of the busing policy;

2. Feelings and attitudes expressed by the parents;

3. Inappropriate reception by the receiving school;

4. No feeling of belonging because the school is not in their neighborhood — not "their school";

5. Feeling of being unwanted in the receiving school; and

6. Feeling that they are being used.

Many of the children feel and act like visitors in their school and act that way, never really settling down to serious academic work unless forced to do so. Some teachers permit this to happen.

Of course, we cannot forget all of the "normal" or "average" students who probably make up the majority of our school population and who go about doing their daily work without exceptions or problems. For the most part, these students like their schools, teachers and the friendships they have developed, enjoying themselves as they go through the grades.

Every classroom is composed of children who probably have one or more of the characteristics of the students described in the past few pages. There is no such thing as strictly homogeneous grouping if we remember to take into account the unique characteristics of individual children. Moreover, I doubt that there are strictly homogeneous sub-groups within classrooms. So, how do we put children into classes and sub-groups? It depends upon who does the grouping and what qualities that person sees as being important. Some common reasons for assigning children to classes are: parent requests; teacher recommendations; a child's desire to be with friends in the same class; a teacher's relationship with a parent; "political" demands; a teacher's disciplinary tactics; family attachments; and racial quotas. You can see clearly that these reasons have very little, if anything, to do with the teaching and learning process. Yet, the atmosphere for learning is the most important criterion to use in organizing classrooms. Instead of the reasons mentioned, it seems as if more emphasis and time need to be placed on teacher-pupil relationships, matching teaching styles with children's learning styles, as well as the flexibility of the teacher in working with diverse personalities. After all, teachers who find themselves weak in these areas will experience limited success with their classes.

CHAPTER II

Who is Doing the Teaching?

As most prospective employees of any company, institution or organization, applicants for positions in education present themselves with many questions. They also have varying attitudes; levels of experience and expertise; and come from training programs with different educational philosophies, approaches, objectives and expectations of outcomes. Most applicants do a good job of providing information on resumes and applications and during interviews. A few, however, do not see the application process as important—writing letters of application on lined paper torn from spiral notebooks or reporting for interviews totally unprepared.

The process of choosing an applicant generally begins with a review of the resume and application unless oral information has been received via telephone or in person from a supervisor or colleague. Securing references follows if they are not already a part of the application and unless the application contains information that would make the applicant obviously unsuitable for a position. Recommendations from supervisors and colleagues can be the most important part of the application because they evaluate the applicant's past performance and presumably use the knowledge of the applicant's performance potential to note how well the candidate qualifies for the prospective job. Generally speaking, if all recommendations are positive you can feel fairly sure that you have a good applicant. Where you have several recommendations that give disparate evaluations, beware of the possibility that this applicant is not one you should hire. There should be a good reason why you really want to consider a marginal candidate, and in doing so be sure to give the greatest weight to the recommendation of the most recent supervisor and get further information from him or others if possible.

Once you are satisfied that an applicant is the one you want to pursue, you then invite the applicant for an interview. This is the greatest opportunity for applicants to sell themselves, and they should have ample opportunity to do so. After making the candidate comfortable, the interviewer should explain the specific requirements of the job. The discussion and questions should then be directed toward determining whether the candidate possesses the qualifications needed to be effective in the job. Avoid questions that can be answered with "yes" or "no" — the more candidates talk, the more you learn about them. Some suggestions might be to ask candidates to discuss:

1. Their educational philosophy;
2. How they would plan and evaluate certain related activities;
3. How they would teach a concept using different approaches;
4. How they would organize and manage classroom activities;
5. How they would provide for a successful individual learning experience for each child during each class period;
6. How they would make every child feel comfortable in the classroom; and
7. How they would adjust their instruction to make it effective for students on different levels and with different aptitudes and learning styles.

During the question period, most candidates end up with their own questions, and adequate time should be allowed for them to find out more about you and the school in which they expect to work. The interviewer should make sure that the applicant leaves with printed material covering any important information not discussed during the interview. Such information can be included in standard information packets kept at interview sites. Although this process might seem to be a bit lengthy, complicated, unnecessary or even confusing, if you expect to be able to choose the best candidates, this is the minimum effort required.

After the interviews comes the really tough decision: which applicants' personal and professional characteristics best match the personalities and learning styles of the students with whom they would be working. I'm sure that we all have heard the old saying that any child should be able to learn from any teacher. This idea is both incorrect and outdated. Unless teaching style and learning style mesh, the learner will suffer.

An experienced examiner should be able to identify and appraise a candidate's individual traits. Some of the specific traits, characteristics or qualities necessary for at least satisfactory service as a teacher are:

1. A pleasing personality,
2. A positive attitude,
3. A satisfactory academic record,
4. Proficiency in the use of the English language,

5. Ability and willingness to work successfully with parents,

6. Ability and willingness to work with other staff members, and

7. The necessary experience or comparable training in and demonstrated knowledge of appropriate methodology.

Even though I have listed several characteristics that I feel are required for a person to be a good teacher, I know of no absolute single or group of characteristics that guarantees success with teaching children. Educators and researchers have spent much energy, time and money studying the effects on learning from lists of teacher characteristics much longer than mine. While these studies have been interesting, they failed to identify how these specific characteristics combine to make a good teacher. However, the one single trait generally agreed upon is that the teacher must be a "good" person.

In the absence of specific personality characteristics and qualities, we are left to determine the rating of a teacher by other means. To begin with, university programs and professors tend not to direct their teaching to the needs of the schools. Many professors have never worked as public or private school teachers and, therefore, have no idea of the schools' real needs. They teach theories they have been taught, which do not necessarily apply in the classroom and attempt to influence future teachers to think as they do. Some teaching educators resent having to teach the courses as prescribed because of their ego problems and do an unsatisfactory job of presenting ideas and materials in a standard manner to future teachers. A few don't even seem to have much of an idea of what to teach. Their organization and presentation of material are not compatible with the reality of the school. There are those who don't keep up to date with changes in their fields. Instead, they continue to read from the same notes, yellowed with age, copies of which can be obtained from former students from years back. Then there are those professors who teach only a few, if any, class sessions, delegating this responsibility to their teacher assistants. These practices are part of the cause of the deficiencies of newly trained teacher candidates and help to perpetuate the problem. Any two graduates of different schools or from two different classes in the same school do not necessarily have the same understanding of what is expected of them in the classroom.

I am not saying that there are no good teachers in the schools, I'm simply pointing out the difficulties that an administrator must overcome in order to find them. These difficulties are not of the administrator's making, but rather the results of many factors that precede his contact with the applicant, causing confusion over what really makes a good teacher and how to select the best candidates. Administrators, in the midst of this confusion, must make decisions on hiring the best teachers available if they expect to have an effective learning program in their school. How do they do it?

In the absence of specific guidelines, administrators must cut through the confusion and rely on a set of criteria which will guarantee a positive interaction between the teacher and students. My primary criterion is whether teaching style matches learning style. This has to be the number one focus if we expect children to learn and teachers to succeed. A bright child placed with the wrong teacher loses interest and can become as much a problem as any other child. Average and slower children only become more uninterested, slower and lost in their frustration. As we already know, these circumstances can lead to more serious problems. With the right teacher, every child can and will stretch his ability as he becomes excited by learning on a higher level and by succeeding in skills he thought he could or would never master.

During my second year as a principal, I began to work closely with two teachers in whom I had become interested because of their prior performance records. I hasten to say that I cannot take the credit or blame for their presence on the staff; they were there when I arrived. I mention them here because I think they represent the kind of teachers we want for our children. As model teachers you would think that they would be similar in personality and teaching style, but in reality they were more like the odd couple. One was a few years away from retirement; the other was much younger. One was black; the other white. One was very conservative, but open-minded and a leader among the staff; the other was a follower at best, although usually quietly pursuing her own ideas. One was a genius at working with parents; the other was not nearly as diplomatic and not particularly popular with parents. One was extremely well organized; the other seemed unsystematic but aware. One was always up to date and punctual; the other needed a bit of prodding.

With these characteristics, and more, you would think that one of the teachers would have a disciplined class environment and the other a free-for-all. But this was not the case. Each of the two teachers used her own personality and ability to work with the children. The result produced standardized test scores (MAT) showing at least two years' progress for each child in both classes for every year over a three-year period. And these were heterogeneously mixed classes. I know that you find it hard or impossible to believe. Well, so did I, in the beginning. So, I set out to find out their secret so that it could be passed on to others. To my surprise, after many, many hours of observation, checking records, interviewing and evaluating their use of materials, it became clear that there was no obvious secret. These teachers had "magical" means of developing effective interaction with the children and motivating them to want to learn. It was obvious that each teacher knew her children well enough to adjust classroom management, activities, curriculum, and presentation style to hold the pupils' interest and maintain high standards. In spite of their differences, these two teachers had one characteristic in common: they refused to let their own personalities and other personal factors interfere with their positive interaction with children. They were both able to adapt their materials and techniques to develop a teaching style best suited for the learning styles of each child in their classes. In addition, these teachers did not teach to standardized test results; they taught basic concepts, which they evaluated through performance objectives as the year progressed and used the results as a means of reporting to parents. This method emphasized what was being learned rather than a mere numerical score — which doesn't accurately describe what a child has learned.

In another school, I had the pleasure of working with a super group of teachers on a different level. This school was experimenting with teaching a newly developed activity-based science program in classes meeting several times per week. The number of classes was determined by the type and level of the children in each class. The program was highly structured and organized but left ample room for the teacher to make adjustments as needed for greater effectiveness.

When the program was introduced, the staff of mainly young inexperienced teachers was apprehensive. However, with the exception of one, the teachers were smart, eager to learn, anxious to become good teachers, cooperative, enjoyed working with the pupils in the school and liked working with each other. They were an energetic group who viewed the implementation of the program as a challenge and a chance for personal success. To get them started, we distributed materials and conducted workshops to acquaint them with required classroom organization, procedures, equipment and some basic teaching techniques used in the program. They went through the training with enthusiasm and looked forward to beginning to teach the new curriculum.

After a short time, some very interesting things began to happen. Because of the newness of the program, they started

33

to help each other by sharing ideas and materials and often spent planning time together. Together they previewed the new material and tested experiments and activities for accuracy and workability. Those teachers working with children on the same grade level formed small sub-groups so that they could be more specific in sharing their ideas. In the department we had a practice requiring each teacher to observe all of his or her colleagues in the department during the school year. These teachers willingly cooperated and even issued challenges to each other to see who could do a better job of teaching the lesson in question. In addition, they invited other teachers in the department to observe lessons that they felt they taught extremely well or with which they needed help. The chairman was also invited and asked for input from his observations and hosted each teacher in his classroom for at least one lesson. Planning required a great deal of imagination and pride, and the teachers even employed ideas from other subject areas to ensure that each child was actively involved in every lesson. Some teachers were energetic enough to type their plans and draw their experiment diagrams in color. The teachers' lounge became foreign territory to this staff who spent their free time in the chairman's office and laboratory consulting about the program, enjoying each other and building friendships.

A third exemplary group of teachers whom any principal would enjoy working with had the challenge of opening
a junior high school (grades 7-9) in the middle of the school
year, located in the middle of an urban "gangland." By the
time I joined the staff most of the "weak" teachers had been
discharged or transferred and "stronger" teachers hired in
their places. In fact, I joined the staff to replace one of those
"weak" teachers whose class was so disruptive that a student
had thrown a chair out of a third floor window.

The principal of this school was a tiny lady, not more
than five feet tall and probably weighing no more than a
hundred pounds. She was a highly competent professional
who could take over and effectively teach any class in the
school. And she required every teacher to do the same. She
had the highest standards for both students and teachers,
but was fair to students and supportive with teachers. You
could not ask for a better person to work with parents. She
was also a natural diplomat in working with adamant, threatening and/or disruptive parents.

In this school, I don't believe that there was a single per-
manent teacher who was unhappy or did not do his or her
best to be effective with every class. When new teachers were
assigned to the school, the staff took them "under their wings"
and made sure that they understood and could properly

implement procedures, rules, curriculum, standards and other aspects of school operation. Some of the more specific teaching strategies of the teachers included:

1. Being present at the classroom door to welcome children as they arrived.
2. Planning activities for children to do as soon as they entered the room.
3. Demonstrating respect for and acceptance of students.
4. Maintaining high academic and behavior standards at all times.
5. Organizing the classroom and planning activities to ensure that each child had an appropriate learning experience during each class period.
6. Remaining after school hours to do extra work with students, work with other staff members or have conferences with parents.
7. Volunteering to supervise clubs after regular school hours.
8. Refusing to discuss problems or gossip about students in either the lounge or the cafeteria.
9. Communicating with parents by any means, even visiting their students' homes.

10. Spending time with other staff members to develop closer working relationships.

11. Supervising the hallways between classes.

Overall, this group of teachers was the best staff I have ever seen assembled under one roof. Each one had either an M.A. or M.S. or 30 graduate credits from an accredited university. Many had much more. Without a doubt, they were doing what they wanted to do and enjoying it. They had no quarrel with the requirements of the job as long as they understood its purpose. They had tremendous respect for each other, and many close friendships developed from their working interactions. Because of their expertise and maturity as teachers, the majority of the members of this staff earned higher positions in supervision and administration during their careers. It might be noteworthy to mention that a student from that school became motivated enough to complete school and become superintendent of schools for that city.

Teaching is an extremely hard job to do effectively. Many applicants see this as an easy way of making a living, earning benefits, getting many vacation days and being mainly dispensers of information. Those who enter the profession with these beliefs quickly find that their perceptions were incorrect, and they either had to make corrections or change professions. There are teachers who, for various reasons, stay in the profession without commitment or adequate knowledge for the duration of their careers — harming children all along the way. I know of a teacher whose evaluation indicated that she was deficient in certain areas even after many years of teaching. She refused to agree with or sign the evaluation, saying that she knew she was a good teacher. The evaluator then requested that she be transferred. Because of connections with the right people, nothing happened and she continued the same practices. Fortunately, her case isn't typical, but similar situations happen far too often.

I believe that the majority of school systems across the country can use more good teachers in most subject areas. If a prospective teacher feels that he or she will fit into the profession, he or she will find the experience very rewarding if done right. However, I caution any teacher applicant or already established teacher to avoid some common, negative practices used by both regular and substitute teachers. Some examples are:

1. Allowing unlimited talking at the beginning of the class period and telling the class, "I've got mine. You have to get yours".

2. While waiting for the class to get quiet at the beginning of the period, telling the class, "When you are ready, we will get started".

3. Sitting at the desk reading the paper while the class is basically unsupervised and out of control.

4. Making children copy extensive notes from the chalkboard, particularly if the ideas haven't been explained.

5. Having children fill in stacks of dittoed worksheets.

6. Making children read a chapter in the textbook and answer the questions at the end without prior discussion of content and identifying the children's specific questions.

7. Not demonstrating how abstract concepts are applied.

I urge anyone entering the profession to avoid these negative practices and master the correct and positive procedures mentioned throughout this chapter. Adopting the positive procedures and acquiring a positive attitude will net great dividends. The good principal will use his or her best judgment to determine whether to hire and retain teachers, based upon information indicating that the candidate possesses positive personal and teaching characteristics and continues to develop them.

CHAPTER III

What is Being Taught?

While there is much talk and concern about education on the national level, most decisions concerning programs and practices are made on the state level. Of course, there are those federally funded programs that are controlled by national regulations.

Generally, states have an education department, which, along with their state superintendent, has the responsibility of determining what should be taught in the public schools of all school districts. The source, content and format of the material may, and probably will, vary from state to state. Some states may simply choose textbooks and require that the books be followed very closely. Some decide upon areas to be taught and try to buy textbooks that supplement the basic material. Some state systems just develop general outlines and leave the individual school districts to interpret them and fill in the details. Sometimes school systems purchase commercial programs and require that they be used in certain subject areas. Committees on the state or local level, or groups of state and local personnel may also develop materials. These materials are generally presented to schools and designated as a syllabus or a uniform curriculum for each subject area. The curricula outline goals, courses and possibly materials needed to teach the material but leave it up to the teacher to complete the details necessary to develop and teach the individual lessons. A syllabus takes much of the work out of planning by presenting the material in basic lesson plan form. Both formats are helpful in guiding teachers through a course of study and may also leave room for innovations, but a syllabus gives greater assurance that all children are exposed to the same material.

Even though the curriculum is the blueprint for instruction in a school or school system, there are those teachers and administrators who believe that it is not needed and actively fight its implementation in their schools. Although they give many reasons that seem logical to them, the real reasons appear to be the fear of accountability and the desire to "do their own thing," whatever that may be.

Whether a school or system decides to use a particular

41

syllabus or curriculum, they must ensure that it has been developed with the needs of the children in mind. One of the first things to be considered is the type of children for whom you are planning. The materials and books must be in a form that these children can read and familiarize themselves with easily — often these are simple home-made materials or things the student sees or uses in his or her home, on the farm or in his or her daily activities. When it comes to teaching ideas, use the simplest down-to-earth examples in order to be in tune with the children's experiences and developmental level. Secondly, the plan for pupil activities should be actually feasible in the classroom. The term "class work" should really be meaningful for every class period. Ensure that every child makes a contribution during every class period. Make some allowances for the fact that children perform on different levels. Plan enrichment activities for gifted children, rather than place them on a higher grade level. Ensure that every child is exposed to the same material even if it means making adjustments for individuals or groups. Ready-made programs usually do not provide for this.

During the time I worked as a classroom teacher and department chairman, I had the pleasure of working with a curriculum committee over a period of four years. Our goal was to develop a science syllabus for slow inner city seventh, eighth and ninth grade children. We developed this special set of materials because the prevailing opinion was that these pupils could not learn the material required in the regular syllabus. The director of science for the system felt strongly that the pupils in question could learn the same concepts over a longer period of time with the adaptation of some materials and methods of presentation.

Our committee, made up of eight teachers and a supervisor, was responsible for choosing the material and methods included in the syllabus. We started with the regular syllabus and determined how the same material could be divided into six periods per week instead of four. Each subgroup of two teachers worked in one of the major areas: biology, chemistry, earth science or physics. My partner and I found a great challenge in planning the area of biology. One of the greatest challenges was to accept, check out and/or choose textbooks to ensure that the content was adequate, the reading level was appropriate and that the presentation of the material was at least satisfactory. In the course of this project, we were astounded to find that books contained so many errors in content and in the presentation. Demonstrations and some experiments, which have become classics over the years, are still being taught. Since this syllabus was being developed as an activity based program (four children working together), we had to develop worksheets which we were sure everyone could read, understand and follow. We had to make sure that the animals and plants they worked with were familiar to them. An example might be to dissect a fish instead of a frog and a pinto bean instead of a lima bean. The reason for such changes is that many inner city children are not familiar with the frogs or lima beans used in the regular syllabus. The main point is to teach a concept using the materials with which the pupils are most familiar. These materials can be changed depending upon the community in which you work or the type of children you teach. We had to make many other changes that are too numerous to list here.

In order to ensure that a new syllabus is valid, it must be tested in the classroom. In this case, teachers were teaching the material in the syllabus as it was being written or shortly thereafter. Members of the curriculum committee were teachers of the program in their schools, also serving as consultants and supervisors for other teachers. Every week, or even more frequently, we met as a group with our supervisor to discuss our progress, failures and future plans. Any pair of writers was always glad to share ideas with the other three pairs. We spent many evenings trying to figure out how to get an idea across to the pupils at their level of understanding or how to make an experiment work the way it should. Our director felt very strongly about what we were doing and would not accept anything less than what he felt would be understood and workable everyday in the classroom. That is the standard by which all curricula should be measured.

During the period in which I started teaching, it was common to have different groups of pupils on the same grade level taught from separate syllabi. This was not being done undercover but as an accepted practice known as tracking. It was generally in practice more in schools or areas in which there was a sizeable number of "slow" children who were allegedly holding back so-called "brighter" children. As time passed and the more we learned about teaching, it became obvious that such a practice was not necessary or even desirable. I do not agree with the use of tracking in our public schools.

Even though tracking is not an acceptable practice, I had an eye-opening experience of tracking in the last school where I was the principal. While tracking was not an organized, official program in that K-5 school, it was alive and well in actuality. I first became aware of de facto tracking when I attempted to assign children to classes. The school put tracking into practice because the prior principal had permitted a small group of demanding parents to have their choice of teachers on each grade level. These teachers had become accustomed to having only children from privileged homes in their classes. They were as much politicians as teachers and found it difficult to work with other children. Because of this, I had to make some major adjustments. Individual problems of this nature can be found throughout school systems and individual schools, particularly where teachers, principals and parents don't work cooperatively in accordance with established, acceptable practices.

During the early 80s, I was working in a school system that was undergoing some major changes in programs, integration, busing and staff training. The plans for integration required that black children be bused from the inner city to suburban schools and that white children be bused into inner city schools. After developing elaborate plans to carry out his proposal, the superintendent was never able to get support for it either from white suburban parents or the board of education. As the result of this strong conflict, the superintendent was forced to leave his position and the board began to search for someone who had a plan that would integrate the schools but would not force the white parents to send their children to inner city schools.

After conducting a nationwide search, the board hired a superintendent who they felt would support an integration program that would eliminate the problem of forcing the white children to attend inner city schools. The new superintendent sold them the idea of magnet schools. The basic concept of the magnet program was to make the inner city schools so attractive that white parents would want to send their children to them. The magnet program required a total reorganization of the school system and major changes in philosophy and practices. To begin with, principals were not assigned but instead were asked to volunteer to serve in these schools. The magnet principals were then permitted to raid the staff of any school and hire any teacher so long as the teacher agreed to the change. Money and materials earmarked for regular schools were diverted to magnet schools. Massive reassignments of children were necessary, as well as the buses to get them to and from these magnet schools. The magnet school staffs met separately with their own supervisor as if they were a separate system. In essence, they were a separate group who created ill feelings throughout the system.

I was one of those magnet school principals, but I don't believe that any of us fully realized what we were in for until it was too late to back out. I felt that the process and philosophy were clearly being followed with regard for only those parents who didn't want to send their children to inner city schools and at the expense of the rest of the district. In a staff meeting when this was discussed, I remember offering the alternate solution of enriching all of the schools so that all children would receive additional benefits. I was told emphatically that they did not want the programs equalized because the magnet schools would lose their drawing power.

In my judgment, magnet schools represent just one more method of tracking and "dividing and conquering." These schools get the best staff, more and better materials, more special programs and more transportation services. If my memory serves me right, one school had 72 buses delivering children on a daily basis. I guess you can tell that I do not like magnet schools, particularly because of their philosophy, the drain they put on other schools in the district and the image they create for a system. I am also convinced that magnet school programs on the elementary and middle school levels do not provide as much time for instruction in the basics as "regular" schools.

There are many good ideas that never reach the schools or classrooms because of the attitudes of supervisors, politicians and the people controlling the purse strings. It is not uncommon for politicians or supervisors to force bad programs into schools or refuse to let good ideas be implemented because of personal reasons, including jealousy, fear of losing control or unwillingness to give credit for an idea to someone else. I observed an example of this operating method one year while I was principal of a K-5 school. I was given an "extra" teacher to enrich my programs as I had requested for the second half of the year. The program was planned and put into operation immediately and was so successful that it got the attention of my supervisors and administrators, the superintendent and the local media, all of whom gave positive feedback on the results. In order to have the program continued the following year, I had to go through the office of a supervisor who had not been involved with the original plan. Guess what! I didn't get the approval and I had to cancel the program. This supervisor gave me the run-around for the entire summer before canceling the program at the last minute on the grounds that money was not available to pay for the extra teaching position. While that would have been a valid reason, if it were true, later in the year the basic idea of the program was reportedly being implemented in another school using different staff members.

Another example that comes to mind concerns the need for providing more time to work with each child in every class. My staff and I did some creative school-wide scheduling that would do just what teachers had been talking about and requesting without the addition of new staff or additional money. The new organization would have required more precise grouping, team teaching and planning, greater cooperation among all staff and more detailed planning for the individual child. When we presented the new schedule to the staff, reactions ranged from very negative to very positive, depending upon individual, group and teacher organization perceptions. Apparently, because the implementation of this program would have required a bit more than the average teacher was willing to give, a group of teachers collectively convinced the superintendent not to use the plan in the school. Unfortunately this action also stopped the debate about the plan to provide for more individualized instruction. The losers in both cases were the children, who had nothing to say in either case. They are always the ones who suffer when we let our personal, selfish or prejudicial feelings affect what we do in working with them.

When I was a classroom teacher, I took great pride in making detailed lesson plans for each period. This gave me the assurance that I was teaching everything that needed to be covered. To my surprise, I noticed that some of those perfectly planned lessons turned out to be perfect flops as far as the pupils were concerned. On the other hand, some of my lessons, which were barely outlined and more spontaneous, generated much more enthusiasm and involvement than the most well planned activities or lessons.

In working with teachers who used a teacher's guide to help teach a reading or math series, I discovered that they tended to use the guide as the "bible" and followed it without any deviation, regardless of the type of class or child they were teaching, even if the series only gave unit goals or objectives for the hypothetical, or "average" child. My concern and emphases were: to (a) have teachers divide the unit goals or objectives into daily or individual goals that were appropriate for the children in the class; and (b) to ensure that the daily or individual objectives were adjusted to meet the needs of the particular class.

If we expect to teach children effectively, we must know them well enough to be able to choose the appropriate materials and equipment that will motivate them and keep their interest sufficiently for them to grasp the concept being taught. Teachers must keep in mind the need for flexibility, adjustment and modification while planning so that lessons will always meet the needs, interests and, most of all, the learning styles of the children. Without this, we risk losing the pupils' attention and desire to remain with the class.

Companies that produce and print educational materials are constantly knocking at your door attempting to sell ideas and materials that presumably will do a better job than what you are doing. As you listen to them, if you do, keep in mind that:

1. These companies are in business to make money.
2. These materials are developed for mass appeal, not specifically for your school system or your classes.
3. These materials were probably not developed by educators.
4. It will take time for you to study, use and evaluate the new material.
5. You will have to use valuable instruction time to explain the new materials to the pupils.

As an alternative to purchasing new, sophisticated teaching materials of questionable value, we need to remember that pupils learn better when using materials with which they are familiar. Think back to how young babies are happier playing with pots and pans than with the new store-bought toys. The same goes for equipment and materials used in the classroom. The level of learning, interest and participation will be consistently higher if we use familiar instructional materials.

I'm sure that you have heard at least one pupil question why he or she had to learn the material you are teaching. Many boys and girls are currently on the streets because they did not get a satisfactory or correct response. If we fail to show how the material is relevant or applied, the rest of the teaching process becomes useless to the pupil.

CHAPTER IV

How is Teaching Being Done?

If you spend much time in the hallways near the entrance to classrooms, you will sometimes hear, "Come in, sit down and shut up!" directed to children entering the room. The use of that statement gives me the feeling that the teacher in question is lacking in certain aspects of classroom management. I also get the impression that the teacher needs help in defining his/her role and responsibilities in preparing children for instruction, something that should have been done at the beginning of the year.

It is impossible to outline specifically here everything a teacher needs to do in the classroom at the beginning of the period. However, here are some of the important functions a teacher should perform in order to be successful with the children in his/her class. The teacher should:

1. Be stationed at the entrance to the room as the children enter.
2. Welcome each child to the room in a pleasant manner.
3. Make each child feel comfortable in the room without any sign of prejudice.
4. Accept each child as he/she is and make efforts to improve him/her.
5. Make each child feel that he/she is a part of the classroom program.
6. Help the children in developing a positive self-concept.
7. Help those children who need help in developing confidence in work and behavior.
8. Teach the children how to relate to each other.
9. Use the zero base level for beginning instruction in all subject areas.
10. Plan instruction for the full class period.

All of the above actions, and more, need to be taken the first time the teacher meets with the class and repeated every meeting thereafter if needed. As the teacher practices going through these actions, they should become automatic as a part of his/her preparation and daily procedure.

Many teachers seem to feel that children should come to

HODN

school self-disciplined, already motivated and take their seats like little robots ready to absorb the information, usually given in lecture form. Teachers often see themselves mainly as information dispensers with the primary role of talking at, rather than interacting with the pupils. While this might be most comfortable for some teachers, it is probably the least effective of all the teaching styles, methods or approaches. I do not believe that lecturing should be used, except in special cases, because it generally is boring, nor does it give any feedback that would indicate whether pupils are learning.

While there are many styles or methods of teaching, there is one which I favor and used during my tenure in the classroom. This activity-based program can be used on all grade levels and in any subject area. It requires that every pupil take an active part in the class, or a lab. The teacher is mainly an energizer and a guide. Each pupil gets the chance to do something successful each day and, depending upon the class, gets the chance to perform each task required in the lesson.

I will attempt to describe the program by explaining how it was used in a junior high school Science class. The classrooms had 16 double desks screwed to a wooden floor. Two pupils sat at each double desk facing the front of the room. After going through the motivational activity and indicating that they understood the worksheet (required for laboratory work), the two pupils sitting at each of the four front and third row desks would turn around to the desks behind them to form eight desks with four pupils at each desk. The pupils in each group were given a number (1, 2, 3 or 4) for the duration of the course. One of the four pupils held the position of chairperson for his/her group for a period of a week on a rotation basis. The duties of the chairperson were to make sure that:

1. required materials were present on the desk;
2. the other three students had what they needed, were following instructions, completing the worksheet and reporting their findings;
3. safety procedures were followed; and
4. he/she reported the group conclusion to the teacher.

The class discussed the conclusions and the class recorder wrote outcomes on the chalkboard so the class could include them in their notebooks.

Along with, or as a part of the activity-based program, we employed some of the following principles:

1. All pupils were given the clear understanding that coming to school was their job, just as their parents went to work each day. Further, they were required to do their class work on a daily basis and were not

permitted to sit in class for a full period doing nothing.

2. We required that pupils begin thinking about the lesson by focusing on a "thought question" we had written on the chalkboard before they entered the room. This helped with their motivation and allowed them to deduce the aim of the lesson.

3. We organized the classroom so that pupils had a maximum chance to be involved in all activities. To partly achieve this aim, we:

   a. appointed a committee to keep the bulletin boards current with appropriate materials;

   b. appointed a class recorder to write notes on the chalkboard in language pupils understood;

   c. assigned a reference person to look up answers in desk references when answers were unknown; and

   d. used pupils to explain difficult concepts in their own language.

There is no limit to the principles you may apply to a lesson or a program to keep children involved.

The activity-based program can be used in all subject areas. It does not have to be limited to use in science experiments or in a cooking class. The key to this approach is having activities in which the pupils become involved. This involvement can range from answering questions to evaluating someone else's answer to playing a position on a ball team. In fact, I recommend that the teacher use applicable activities from any and all subject areas for a richer and more interesting program. An additional way to boost interest and involvement is to use class-made or homemade materials, and well-known activities always help to liven up a lesson and improve learning.

Fast-talking salespeople offering attractive commercial programs and teaching materials frequent schools and classrooms attempting to sell their equipment and materials to teachers. These programs do not necessarily fit into the material being currently taught or in the curriculum in general. But many teachers seem to feel that the more gadgets or materials they have in their room, whether they apply to their program or not, the better teacher they are. These are the teachers whom salespeople prey upon and who can waste money designated for supplies and materials.

Materials and supplies need to meet acceptable criteria whether they are to be used as replacements or additions to a curriculum or program. Some questions to ask when deciding how to spend money for supplies and enhancements are:

1. Will this material fulfill a need in my program?

2. Will this material replace an old item, or be used to enrich my program?

3. Will it change the outcomes of my current program?

4. Is the item on the right grade level?

5. Does the material require extensive training in order for pupils to use it?

6. Will this item withstand use–and abuse–by pupils?

7. Has this material been tested and proven to be effective?

In choosing materials and equipment for any class or program, you must be sure that the items fit into your program and that they can be adapted to the level and needs of the class.

Many schools and systems, particularly if they are having performance problems, become involved in controversial new programs that have little chance for success, to say the least. Responsible people promise future success without really knowing what to expect. As a program begins to fail to produce the promised results, publicity about it gradually decreases until the program is finally quietly discontinued. Some districts or systems show great interest in commercial programs, probably thinking that these programs can do what they have not been able to do — teach the children.

In my judgment, those people who constantly purchase programs to solve their teaching-learning problems do not understand that programs do not teach children, teachers do. So, if I am correct, the answer to many learning problems can be found in teacher training. This means equipping teachers with proper methods of presentation of material so that they get both the required educational results as well as effective interaction with the many pupils who do not relate well to authority. It appears that teachers depend too much on textbooks, workbooks and other programmed material, without making any adaptations for the children in their classes. Overuse of worksheets is just assigning busy work. Teachers give assignments from textbooks without having first discussed the topic in class. Talking and listening as a method of teaching is seldom used among students because of infrequent classroom discussions and partly because of the teacher's lack of confidence in controlling such groups.

Not so long ago teachers were given a curriculum guide, a teacher's edition of the textbook and a few other items, depending upon the subject, for a class of 30+ children. Computers were not available, slide rules and estimating were not permitted in math, wall charts and other audio/visual aids were limited and scheduled for classroom use. There was, however, plenty of chalk for the chalkboard. With these limited materials, teachers set some high standards and motivated children to achieve at high levels.

Listening and talking are two of the basic ways we communicate and learn. They are the two ways that were primarily used in the absence of the many high tech aids in classrooms today. However, in order for teachers to use class discussion in teaching today, they must establish standards and develop procedures to help pupils interact with each other. It becomes extremely important to establish with the pupils that whatever they have to say is important and, if this is so, everyone else except the talker should be listening. It is also very important that pupils understand and accept the fact that each pupil might have unique understandings or feelings about issues and that everyone has a right to express those feelings. In addition, we need to develop the understanding that a healthy attitude is produced by exchanging ideas as long as we concentrate on the issues and not get involved in personalities.

In order for teachers to use class discussion as a means of teaching, they must be confident of their abilities, be guidance-minded, help pupils to develop respect for each other and other opinions, and to teach the procedure for holding an effective discussion. These things can be taught as you teach regular lessons that require a lot of discussion through effective questioning technique. Some of the specifics of this technique are:

1. Do not call on only the pupils who always have their hands raised. This gives every pupil the feeling and the chance to be a part of the lesson.

2. Ask the question first and then call on the pupil you want to answer. This keeps pupils from "tuning out" because they do not know who will be expected to answer.

3. Insist that the pupil answering the question talk to the class not directly back to the teacher. This helps to draw the rest of the class into the lesson.

4. Do not accept the first answer given and do not call it right or wrong. Keep the original question alive by asking several pupils questions such as: "What do you think, Joe?", "What is your explanation, Jane?" and "Why is Jane correct, Jerry?". Limit the responses according to available time and other factors.

5. Ask different individual pupils to identify important points covered in the lesson and give reasons why they are important.

6. Using the procedure outlined, have pupils develop a summary for inclusion in their notebooks.

7. Avoid asking questions that may be answered with

"yes" or "no". These questions discourage conversation.

While this appears to be a very simple method, it requires that the teacher have self-confidence and train the pupils. It may also test your patience since you will have to repeat the procedure for an unknown number of times until it becomes automatic with both you and the pupils. Then you will begin to enjoy some of the qualities you never thought your pupils possessed. All pupils can and should participate successfully in class discussions, since they help to formulate the very basis for learning.

Every day thousands of children go home and tell parents that nothing happened in school. The same day older children congregate on street corners or in other places after "cutting" classes or not going to school at all. While younger children sit in class and daydream, go to the bathroom frequently or get in trouble doing other things they should not do, older pupils frequently form groups and get in trouble outside of the classroom and school. This behavior can range anywhere from simple loitering to serious felonies and drug use. I like to think that good teaching could be a big factor in preventing these behaviors. If pupils were really interested in classroom activities, they would not want to leave them or "create" other activities to occupy their time.

I do not believe that I have worked with or seen any pupils who do not want to learn. However, I have seen many cases where it becomes hard to keep young pupils on task for any length of time without something else grabbing their attention. On many occasions older pupils have asked why they had to learn certain material. Many get a good answer but many do not. We can increase this level of interest in our daily lessons by including describing how the concept is used in business, homes and daily living. In addition to classroom activities, homework assignments and projects can contribute greatly to an appreciation of how abstract concepts are practical. An example might be to have young pupils locate, name and give the function of all simple machines in their home after teaching a lesson or unit on the subject. Another example might be to have math pupils visit a building site to learn how math (geometry & trigonometry) is used in construction. A third example might be to have a group put together a model to help them understand the importance of reading, following directions and measuring correctly. Whatever the abstract concept is, it must be explained in terms of its application as a part of the lesson.

Children old and bold enough to leave school need a bit more attention and special help. Not only do they find the classroom boring, but they think that they don't need school at all. Yet they all desire success as much as the so-called regular college-bound pupils. For students who simply do not want to go to college, we don't provide enough alternatives for them in the public schools. We continue to hold on to the antiquated idea that every child wants to and will become a doctor, lawyer, teacher or other professional who graduates from a four year college with a bachelor's degree. We almost forget all other courses of study although many of the students who avoid school would love to be taking courses in these areas. I believe that these pupils need to be provided for as well as all of the others. I also believe that our junior and senior high schools should become comprehensive schools (offering academic and technical courses) so that all students would have an equal chance for success in an area of their choice. I believe that comprehensive curricula would cut the drop-out rate to practically zero with more pupils learning how to make a living rather than burdening society.

Just as every lesson needs an aim or objective, it needs a summary. When children report to parents that nothing happened in class on a given day, it's because they really don't know what the final outcomes of lessons were since their teachers didn't give summaries. As teachers, we assume that as long as we cover the material during the period, the pupils automatically understand what the important points were. Since summarizing is the easiest part of the lesson, there is hardly any reason for omitting it. Not only should teachers always give summaries, but also the students should record them in the notes for the day.

Homework, probably the most controversial part of a lesson, gets more discussion than any other aspect of teaching. Some people say it should be eliminated while others think it should be increased. Some parents feel that teachers who don't assign a lot of homework are bad teachers; others don't want to have to help pupils with the extra work. Some schools and school systems have gone so far as to make special policies covering the use and assignment of homework. Teachers, for the most part, disregard the policies and use homework according to their own philosophy and needs.

I feel that the purpose of homework is to supplement what has been taught in the classroom. Pupils and parents need not go through the daily stress of getting homework done if teachers followed certain guidelines in the classroom.

1. Assign homework only when it is necessary, not just because it's another day.
2. Make homework assignments an extension of what was taught in school the same day.
3. Never give homework as a punishment.

4. Collect and correct homework.

5. Make homework assignments as practical as possible.

6. Homework should be work that pupils can do without having to do extensive research at home or the library.

7. Don't give homework in an area that hasn't been taught in class. For example: reading the next chapter in the textbook and answering the ten questions at the end.

Homework can be a positive, enjoyable part of lessons for teachers, parents and pupils if some of the stress is removed from it.

CHAPTER V

How Do We Evaluate Teaching?

Many teachers are rated as "excellent," "good" or "bad," depending upon the type of children they teach. If they have a "smart" class, they are rated as an "excellent" teacher; a slow class makes them a "poor" or "bad" teacher. Many parents appear to have this feeling and request certain teachers for their children using this thinking as a guideline. Even some supervisors and administrators make the mistake of assigning children to classes based upon this very unscientific type of rating.

Some teachers expend a lot of energy attempting to find out what parents like so that they can model their program and methods accordingly. They encourage and accept suggestions from parents on a formal and informal basis. Parents work in the classroom and go on trips to assist teachers with teaching duties. They help teachers with correcting homework, written assignments, lunchroom duty and other activities while taking mental notes of what kind of teachers they are and whether their child(ren) are working or would work well with them in the future. Teachers generally know these parents well and feel assured that the perception of these parents will reach the ears of the official evaluator. Teachers are also aware that if they don't do pretty much what the parents like negative evaluation points may be forthcoming.

Some supervisors and administrators who evaluate teachers utilize the information from parents as a means of influencing teacher ratings. While some parent observations and opinions are valid, the evaluator often disregards them. It is the evaluator's responsibility to review all input but to be objective in choosing what he or she uses or rejects.

Today, it seems as if almost everyone, except educators, has become an expert on education, teaching and learning. Politicians evaluate school systems and promise to correct deficiencies. Businesses evaluate school systems to determine the location of plants or office centers. Real estate brokers use their evaluations to determine the marketability of homes within certain school districts. And know-it-all parents and community members attempt to control the organization and operation of the schools.

Some people regard teaching and learning as two separate processes. It is often said that children were taught but just didn't learn. On the other hand, there are those who believe that if the pupil does not learn, teaching has not taken place. Both are right in a sense. It is possible for teachers to cover material in a manner that the pupils don't understand. And yet, they claim that they taught the material since it was covered. In my judgment, teaching has not taken place unless the teacher has presented the material in a manner that the pupils can understand. So, it becomes the responsibility of teachers to know the learning styles of their pupils and use that information to determine how to present material. It is a difficult task to know pupils well enough to make those adaptations and to adjust presentations to match their learning styles. I have made some suggestions on preceding pages, but I am including further suggestions below to make it a bit easier for teachers to be more effective.

   a. Take time to get to know the pupils.

   b. Accept pupils as they are without prejudice.

   c. Get to know their likes and dislikes.

   d. Learn their individual talents.

   e. Pay particular attention to how they work.

   f. Notice social patterns and who is friendly with whom.

g. Keep an ear open to detect problems and an open mind and willingness to help.

h. Be available to discuss progress with parents frequently, if needed.

i. Ensure that each pupil actively participates in classroom activities.

j. Notice how pupils work independently.

k. Present material in different ways.

Teachers effectiveness will diminish to a great extent if they fail to identify and use pupils learning styles in their daily classroom activity.

But more than pupils' learning styles must be considered in teacher evaluations. Outlined below are some guidelines that form part of a complete evaluation.

1. Aim of lesson

   a) Should be stated as a question.

   b) Should be elicited from the pupils.

2. Motivation

   a) Should be used to focus interest on the concept of the lesson.

   b) Can be in many forms — verbal, demonstration, etc.

3. Materials
   a) Should be appropriate to help demonstrate concepts.
   b) Must be simple enough for children to use.

4. Procedure
   a) Is the teacher's knowledge adequate?
   b) Does he or she use questions effectively?
   c) Are teacher-pupil interactions positive and effective?
   d) Is presentation of material adequate and varied?

5. Planning
   a) Are materials appropriate?
   b) Is the lesson completed without rushing?

6. Organization
   a) Is the room orderly and clean?
   b) Do pupils carry out assignments without confusion?
   c) Is students' work displayed?

7. Atmosphere
   a) Are pupils orderly and attentive?
   b) Do they exhibit fear of teacher?
   c) Do pupils appear pleasant and forthcoming with information and responses?

8. Summary
   a) Did pupils give a short statement of what the lesson was about?

It is entirely possible that your evaluator may use a modified version of this outline, but these points can serve as a basis for change.

Evaluation of pupil progress presents a different problem from teacher evaluation. Due to the fact that so many people have expressed differing points of view about the rating of pupil progress, how it should be measured and what the standards should be, there is confusion throughout the nation as to how to treat the problem. In addition, there are some people pushing for end-of-year tests, state-made vs. standardized tests and performance objectives vs. grades.

It's always interesting to see how so many different solutions can occur to solve one simple problem. I find it even more interesting to see how unwilling concerned adults are to work together and to make some necessary compromises. I sometimes wonder whether the concerned, responsible people aren't more interested in preserving their egos, ideologies, commitments to others, or their standing in some group more than they are in the welfare of our children.

I was once teaching in a system when it decided to do away with IQ as a basis for class assignments and level of classroom instruction. But the teachers and some others felt that we could not teach the pupils because we did not know their IQ. After going through a period of orientation and assuring them that they could use their own experience and ability to determine adequate activities for the pupils, the attitude of the teachers gradually changed, and in a short period of time teaching was back to normal.

In another system, I was a staff member when some of the teachers and parents were unhappy with the letter grades reporting system on report cards. After a committee of staff and parents worked cooperatively for a short time, the reporting system was changed so that all factions were satisfied. It is my belief that any problem involving student achievement can be solved just as easily as the two mentioned in these paragraphs.

The subject of vouchers has been around for many years, but I have never heard of or seen a positive report on its implementation in any sizeable area or for an appreciable length of time. Vouchers might sound good in theory but there are so many negatives related to the program that the system loses its attractiveness once you investigate it thoroughly. Some of the problems are:

1. Both public and private schools decide whom they enroll.

2. Space for the pupils is not guaranteed.
3. Private schools can expel pupils they don't want who then must return to public schools.
4. Private and parochial schools are not easily accessible to all children in a district.
5. Transportation to and from these schools is not always available.
6. Many schools stress religion, which parents may not want in a school setting.

I have worked with pupils who have been expelled from parochial school, and it is not an easy job to get them readjusted to public schools.

Requiring pupils to take and pass end-of-year tests in order to be promoted brings into focus many concerns. I don't believe that many people would disagree with or reject end-of-year testing if their concerns could be cleared up and questions answered properly. Here are some of my solutions that I'm sure I share with many others who are concerned about education in America:

1. All pupils should return to neighborhood schools. Most parents of black children who are being bused to schools miles away for integration purposes have little or no relationship with their children's school because the parents have a hard time getting to the

school. In essence, these parents' influence on their children's in-school performance has been cut off.

2. The tendency today is to move more toward schools with special programs such as magnet schools. A better and more equitable procedure is to enrich programs in all of the schools rather than to enrich the special schools at the expense of others. All children deserve to be treated equally.

3. Each school should be assigned a staff of teachers and administrators who have basically the same qualifications. No school should have the luxury of 90% "good" teachers while some other school struggles with 10% "good" teachers. In addition, slow classes should not be given to all the "bad" teachers. If there has to be an imbalance, the slower students need the best teachers the most.

4. Teachers must be retrained to be effective with all types of children. We cannot afford to have teachers who can teach only "advanced" or "slow" children. This amounts to tracking teachers.

5. Teachers must be retrained to understand how to work effectively with parents. Our goal in this area should be to develop a positive, cooperative relationship between staff and parents.

6. The curriculum should be the same on any grade level in the area being tested. Each child should be taught at least the basics with enrichment and remediation as needed.

7. Teachers should use basically the same approach and method of teaching.

8. Equipment and supplies should be the same in each school using the same curriculum. There should be no under-stocked or over-stocked schools.

9. Services provided to the school and classes must not be distributed on an unfair basis.

10. Plans for regular and frequent observations and evaluations must be developed for accountability.

11. Any modifications to the curriculum must be the same in all classes.

12. It's important for pupils to know how to take a test. Therefore, test-taking techniques should be taught although the actual test must not be used.

13. All pupils must take a national standardized test such as the Metropolitan Achievement Test or the California Achievement Test, NOT a state prepared test. State and national tests are entirely different and produce disparate results.

Unless we implement all of these points, plus others, I believe that the test scores will continue to lack much validity and not gain much respect.

In addition to the points mentioned above, there are a few that are major issues that we must consider in making curriculum and teaching adjustments. The first is to understand that pupils learn in spurts, not in an even flow as water runs down a stream. Teachers should take this phenomenon into account when making and reading evaluation reports of children's progress. The slow child can learn basically the same material as average children, but it takes a bit longer for them to do so. Give them the time needed for them to succeed. Test scores should not be the only factor that determines a pupil's rating. Certainly the teacher, who knows the pupils better than anyone else, is in position to evaluate them better than any other person or instrument. The teachers' evaluations must be given first priority with all other information as supplementary.

The final point I want to make in the area of pupil evaluation concerns the reporting instrument. The typical reporting instrument is the report card which children take home several times during the school year. The report card generally gives evaluation ratings in terms of numbers (90, 80, 65) or letters (A, B, C) for each subject area. While parents, in general, seem to be familiar with and accept this report card, they do not understand what these symbols represent in terms of what their child actually did or did not learn. If these parents want to know the details of what grading symbols represent, they have to request a conference with the teacher.

In an earlier chapter (Ch. II), I gave a brief description of a reporting system that provides parents with a detailed report of what their children can or can not do and what they have or haven't learned. Some examples to include on this kind of evaluation are: "Has learned multiplication tables through 5"; "Can identify the main points in a story"; "Can correctly divide written work into paragraphs"; "Has learned all of the elements on the Periodic Chart"; "Has developed muscular strength so that he can do 25 chin-ups"; "Has learned how to mix paints to get a desired color". Obviously, the skills to be included on the report are determined by the grade level and subject matter.

In order for students to reach these learning objectives, teachers must study the curriculum for each grade level in every subject area and stress the objectives of the lessons for each unit. This is a project that can best be done by a committee over an extended period of time. Even so, I believe that this time will be well spent and, in the long run, will save time for teachers.

There is no doubt in my mind that this is the best type of reporting system. Incidentally, for those loyal to the letter or number system, they may be combined with the performance objective system. I have seen this system work and believe that it is the best pupil evaluation system we can offer.

CHAPTER VI

How Do We Work With Parents?

During my thirty-one plus years of working as a teacher and administrator in education, I had the pleasure of working with six different parent communities. These groups were as different as any six different individuals but shared a common concern for their children and devoted considerable energy to ensure that their children had the best education possible. Because of the different personalities in the groups, there was no single way to use in working effectively with all of them.

My first experience was in a poor inner city community where a high percentage of the students were gang members from two rival gangs who constantly fought each other. Most parents held jobs but quite a few were unemployed. Some of the working parents were difficult to contact and were unable or unwilling to come to school when asked to do so. The other parents were equally difficult to get to come for conferences.

So, how did we contact and work with parents of children in this school? At that time, each teacher was expected to visit the home of all of his or her pupils and hold a conference with their parents at least once a year and more often if needed. This even meant making some visits at night or other unusual times when parents were available. You might think that these conferences were unproductive, but, in fact, the parents' concern for their children was high and they cooperated enthusiastically. The major problems here were that most parents could not take time away from jobs to come into school while others did not have means of transportation to get there.

My second experience with a parent community was almost exactly opposite of the first one. Pupils attending the school were, on the average, highly motivated and performed on a high level. Since the school was located in the inner city near multilevel apartment buildings, there were no transportation problems and buses were not needed. A few children came by bicycle but walking, city buses and the subway were the major forms of transportation in the community. The parents were mainly professional and business employees, many of whom occupied high level positions. They did not spend much time in the school during the day but they were not hard to contact and were always willing to provide any assistance teachers requested. If a teacher wanted a conference, all he or she had to do was to notify the parent; the response was 100%. All school events were well attended and many were sponsored by the parents. These parents demonstrated their desire for their children to succeed by supporting school activities and working closely with the staff. The parents expected excellence from the teachers and generally got it.

The next parent group with whom I had the pleasure of working was, in a sense, the ideal group. The parents were mainly energetic young mothers who were available during the day, even though they would come to school with their babies and other young children in tow. The school had only kindergarten and first grade so that the pupils were only slightly older than their siblings were. Since the community was rather small, many of the pupils and parents knew and appeared to like each other. These parents helped the staff in any way they could. All they needed was an invitation and authorization from the school.

Another group was in the same school district as the last group discussed, but in this group more fathers were involved and the pupils were a few years older. The residents of the community included parents in all economic categories, from welfare recipients to millionaires. Even though the total group was heterogeneous, the interest level of the pupils appeared to be the same throughout the community. The PTA president served as a major link between the school and the community. She would meet with school officials at least once a week, report to parents and provide sub-groups or individuals to work on the specific school needs. Mothers made direct contact with teachers to help with individual classroom needs. Fathers were more than cooperative and enthusiastic, helping with sports activities as well as projects in other areas. Teacher-parent interaction was positive and took place on a regular basis.

Probably the most difficult yet most enjoyable interaction I had with a parent group was in a K-5 school reputed to be a "difficult" school. The year I became the principal, it was scheduled to be integrated and therefore undergo major changes in the student population assignments. In addition, we had to draw up bus routes and bus stops. Finally, we had to hire new staff members to accommodate the new pupils. In addition to my normal summer duties, I had endless conferences with individuals and parent groups, prepared a parent handbook, gave tours of the school to explain the school program, discussed individual pupils' learning styles, conducted orientation meetings and notified parents of new student assignments. While exhausting, all of these activities resulted in a unified, energetic and cooperative parent community.

The most disappointing relationship that I have had with a parent group was in another K-5 school. I was asked by the superintendent to take the position of principal in this school after a colleague informed him that the school mentioned in the above paragraph was operating so well anyone could run it. My orders basically were to assume the management of the school and make the changes needed to bring it back up to normal. I was also warned only that there was a little hornet's nest of parents who might prove troublesome. Upon reporting to the school I found:

1. A dirty building in disrepair.
2. No enforcement of rules and policies.
3. Teachers who were happy but irresponsible and doing their own thing.
4. Student tracking by ability.
5. Lack of adequate supervision from a principal who had been at the school for more than 15 years.
6. A small group of parents who were doing just about

what they wanted, often against the wishes of many staff members.

7. Some parents going into classrooms uninvited through side doors so that they didn't have to sign in.

Since the school staff, pupils and parents had become accustomed to doing things the way they wanted to, it was extremely difficult to get anyone to change. The children presented very little, if any, opposition to the changes proposed. The teachers, on the other hand, had become set in their ways and fought me at every turn. When I requested transfers for some teachers, they even used their husbands' political pull with the board of education or the superintendent's office to keep from being transferred. One teacher simply quit when I told her that she would not have the same aide the following year. After using all methods I have mentioned in working with other schools, the small groups of parents still attempted to force me to do their bidding even if it meant violating school policies. When I refused, one of the parents confronted me in a threatening manner feeling confident because of the relationship she and her group had with the superintendent. He was always willing to meet and talk with the parents but never let me know when they met or what they discussed — I had to find out through the grape-vine. When things got to the point that this group of parents attempted to block or destroy everything I was trying to accomplish, I felt that I could no longer work in that situation for fear that I would end up saying or doing something I would regret. As the result, I requested a transfer out of the school. It's unfortunate, but I believe this small group of parents focused their attention on me in an attempt to get revenge for my taking away some of the power they had enjoyed for years. They appeared to be more interested in their own activities than they were in doing what was good for the school. How sad!

It has been said that it takes a village to raise a child. Homes and schools make up a large part of the community and certainly are the major centers of education for the average child. Counting transportation time, pupils spend approximately one third of their time involved in school activities and about one half or more of their waking hours in school. With the time between home and school divided almost equally, it is reasonable to assume that a significant portion of learning can take place at home, using the school as the primary educational center and the home as a supplementary learning station. In some cases, the home may become the primary center. For example, I remember my mother teaching me to read from an ABC book before I was enrolled in school. Parents can help their children by drilling multiplication tables, helping with a paper or analyzing a story. It should be obvious that the school and home must work together in order to develop children's abilities. We must encourage parents to become involved with their children, not necessarily as teachers, but as monitors, supervisors, or in any other way that can help the child complete his work correctly.

I happened to be a principal in a district that was undergoing major changes in curriculum and organization. Our new superintendent had been hired primarily to develop a plan to avoid forcing white suburban parents to send their children to inner city schools to replace black children who were being bused to suburban schools. His basic plan was to reorganize and enrich the programs in the inner city schools to the extent that the white parents would actually request inner city assignments for their children (This was his magnet program discussed briefly in Chapter III.) In order to sell his program, he had to hold many meetings with parents and staff and make appropriate promises to every group. One of the ideas he constantly emphasized with parents was that they, rather than the schools, should be making decisions concerning what happened to their children. It took some time for this new idea to sink in but after a while most people accepted the idea—as they interpreted it—while others totally objected to it. Among those who accepted the idea were the resistant parents, the wait-and-see group, the positive parents and the anxious ones. The anxious parents interpreted the idea as being something I do not believe was intended: parents should not just participate in but control the schools.

The interpretation that parents should control the schools spread to such a degree that it eventually became a major problem throughout the system. Some parents became aggressive, feeling that they had the right to go into the schools and challenge the actions and programs of the staff. Many staff members felt they had to go along with parent proposals because they thought the superintendent had authorized the changes. In my judgment, this was all wrong and shouldn't have been allowed to reach this stage. The central office should have made clear from the beginning that we wanted active participation from parents without permitting them to control school activities. There is a very thin line between the two concepts but that line needs to be drawn clearly if parents and schools are to understand their respective duties and functions.

It is, however, extremely important to have the support and participation of our parents and community. In order to develop the kind of relationships we want, we must have clear and mutual understanding regarding the respective roles of school and community. I have mentioned some methods of doing this in preceding chapters, but another simple method of getting basic information to parents is through a parent handbook. The handbook can be mailed, sent home with children or given out at back-to-school functions. Some examples of information items that might be included follow:

1. School hours,
2. Bus schedules and stops,
3. Seating arrangement on buses,
4. Holidays,
5. Supplementary materials and equipment needed,
6. Classroom routines,
7. Lunchroom schedule and menus,
8. Prices of lunch and payment method,
9. Dress codes, if any,
10. Homework policy,
11. Field trip policy,
12. Physical Education requirements,
13. Identification marks on clothing,
14. Telephone usage,
15. Appointments and conferences with staff,
16. Emergency contacts and procedures,

17. Special events,
18. Standardized test schedule and policy,
19. Volunteering, and
20. Fundraising.

If you take a tour of almost any school, you will find parent volunteers doing various jobs in a professional manner. I doubt that you will notice any difference in the quality of work these people do and that being done by school employees. These parent volunteers who give their time and energy to make life a little better in and around schools perform such functions as:

1. Helping to supervise cafeteria,
2. Filing and/or typing in the main office,
3. Copying material for staff,
4. Supervising field trips,
5. Reading to children,
6. Listening to children reading,
7. Working on projects with individual children or classes,
8. Helping in the media center,
9. Helping the gym teachers during games or competitions,
10. Telling stories to classes or groups,
11. Demonstrating materials or ideas to children,

12. Sharing unusual or interesting experiences,

13. Developing and carrying out plans for fundraising,

14. Developing and serving at classroom parties and

15. Planning PTA activities for the school.

What parents do in a school depends entirely upon staff and parents working together, as long as school policy is not ignored.

No school functions at or close to peak performance without parental support and participation. In order to reach a high level of operation, the school needs to reach out to parents with information about policies, procedures, programs and curriculum. In addition, staff must make a concentrated effort to answer parent questions and clear up any concerns they might have. Finally, parents must be invited to join the school in its effort to provide the best education for their children.

Nevertheless, allowing parents to gain too much control of the school is a serious mistake. It is also inappropriate for staff, parents or a combination of the two, to boycott or undermine the school's efforts to implement an effective and positive program for its children. I trust that this will not happen in your school.

HODN

CHAPTER VII

How Have Politics Affected Education?

The state in which I live elects its state superintendent of public instruction by popular vote for a specific term of office. After serving his term, the superintendent can run for any other office. For example, one of our previous superintendents is currently serving as a congressman. I make these statements mainly to establish that the top educator in the state is chosen according to his party affiliation and popularity within the party and among voters, not necessarily because of his qualifications in education. I am not aware of how long this state has followed this procedure nor how many other states do the same thing.

In the absence of any data to support or refute a claim, I would say that electing the superintendent of schools is not necessarily undesirable. However, I do believe that an elected official would be more obligated to follow his party's program than one more beneficial to the children. So, the elected superintendent's programs and practices would depend either upon the nature of his party's program or on his commitment and willingness to do what is best for the children and the district without regard to party support. Good ideas are not always Republican, Democratic or Independent, but everybody should be happy when an idea works, regardless of its source. Furthermore, all political parties should be working closely together, rather than competing with each other, to ensure that every child gets what he needs.

During political campaigns for just about any office, candidates present some kind of an education program or express strong feelings about some aspect of the teaching and learning process. Some of these programs are good although funds may not be available to implement them; some are not worthy of consideration for the general school population; and some are mentioned just to get the voters' attention or approval with no follow-up. Among the few that are accepted, some are delayed for further evaluation, some run into staffing or other problems and others simply disappear because of lack of interest.

Those programs that are approved by the federal government are, for the most part, difficult to implement at the level of the local school system. One of the primary reasons for this difficulty is that they come with guidelines that are very strict in terms of staffing, space, equipment, materials, paper work, transportation for pupils and other factors. In some cases, the programs cannot be implemented where they are most needed because the school or district can not fulfill the requirements of the guidelines. However, because in most cases schools need money and want to help the children, they make programs, staff, space and other adjustments in order to accommodate the programs. Elementary schools generally have less free space, fewer staff members with time in their schedules and less flexibility for additional special programs. Yet, the need and interest are greater on the elementary level. Consequently, more special programs are generally found in elementary schools.

The number of programs developed to serve the handicapped or disabled child (these are the programs I wish to stress in this chapter) has increased as the handicaps have been identified and programs and curricula have been established to help children with disabilities. When I started teaching in the mid-50s, I remember seeing only one such class in a school of approximately 1800 junior high school students. Today, I do not know the exact number in existence, but I do know that they cover a wide range of specific and general disabilities, including special programs for children who are:

1. Autistic,
2. Hearing impaired,
3. Visually impaired,
4. Emotionally handicapped,
5. Learning disabled,
6. Speech impaired.

I'm sure that with a little thought you will be able to add to the list without any problem. If you wish to have a complete listing, call the director of special programs for your school system.

If parents want their child to receive special education services, they must make it known to their child's teacher. If the teacher agrees, then the application can proceed. Information must be collected from testing and many staff members, depending upon the problem and the classes in which the child is enrolled. This information is given to the intervention committee (this committee might be known by a different name in different school systems) which reviews the information and makes the decision whether to admit the child, keep him or her in his or her present class or provide still other services. Although the members of this committee may vary, the committee generally includes the teacher(s), principal, psychologist, reading teacher, guidance teacher or home-school counselor and special program teacher. In some cases, the parents are invited to the meeting when the committee members discuss the information. The final step is to get the parents' approval, without which, the child remains where he or she is.

Federal guidelines for special programs are generally very strict with regard to funding, criteria for admission of children to programs and teacher accountability. A number of years ago, when I was a teacher and A/V coordinator in a junior high school, I was called into the principal's office early in May. I was reminded that the deadline for ordering equipment for special programs was near and that he definitely wanted to beat that deadline. You see, if the total allowance was not spent during one school year, the funding would be cut accordingly the next year. Only certain types of equipment could be ordered with the funds and, since we really did not need any that year, we still ordered the equipment to ensure that our allowance would not be cut the following year. Since we could not use the equipment in regular classes, the equipment was labeled and simply put into a storeroom.

Every special program class I visited, except one, had a majority of black children. I often wondered how such strict guidelines could lead to such highly segregated classes. Some of my theories include:

1. Since teachers are not forced to recommend pupils for these programs, they keep the white children who created problems in the regular classroom.

2. Many black children do not belong in these classes, but some teachers recommend them because they believe their classes will be more manageable without them.

3. Some teachers have not been trained and don't have the ability or the desire to teach the "special" child in a regular classroom.

4. The guidelines, as strict as they are, give the teacher and committee some loopholes through which they can maneuver.

5. The black parents, who really don't understand the implications of the assignment are "talked into" approving it.

6. Once a child is assigned, very few of them ever return to regular classrooms.

7. Some teachers or other staff members on the committee form coalitions in order to get the results they want.

It is puzzling how the supervising authority can permit such cases to continue year after year without investigating them and making corrections. I also cannot understand why black parents do not apply pressure to the school administration to treat their children as they do the white children.

While federal officials push to make broad changes in education, state and local officials concentrate their efforts on the local school system. Federal officials attempt to change education in general, including the local system. Wherever possible, they try to influence changes in administration, personnel and programs. Fortunately, there is no line relationship between federal and local officials — they operate on a cooperative basis.

State and local superintendents operate on different levels. While they both have similar responsibilities, they work with different staffs and have different controlling groups. The elected superintendent, as mentioned in the beginning of this chapter, is responsible to the electorate and the state board of education. The local superintendent is hired by a local board of education, the members of which are elected by the residents of the local school district. He is responsible for the operation of the local school district and must cooperate with the state superintendent and sometimes even other school districts.

The local board of education, local superintendent and his staff are responsible for the total operation of the local school system. This responsibility covers human resources, programs, teaching, educational outcomes, transportation, etc. in the attempt to provide an effective program for the children enrolled. In providing these programs, differences arise regarding how they should be adapted in order for them to be progressive and effective. When agreements are not easy to come by, when someone has a "pet" project or when someone else has a "hidden agenda," politics can enter the picture in the local school district or via a "suggestion" from a local politician. In the local system, the politicians are mainly the members of the local board of education, the superintendent and his high level associates and assistants. A few of the areas in which politics play a role are:

1. Student transfers,
2. Assignments of teachers and administrators,
3. Hiring practices,
4. Granting of tenure,
5. Evaluations.

Before I say any more about this problem, let me cite a

case regarding the type of environment in which this kind of political maneuvering takes place. A community in which I worked was located in the center of an area where state department offices, colleges and state education department offices abounded. Many of the parents of children who attended these schools were employees of these institutions. In addition, some of the parents of these children were teachers in the local schools. There were many obligations and ties among teachers, administrators and supervisors, as well as with the employees of these institutions. In addition, unemployed parents often worked in and visited the schools for the purpose of getting information to use for or against the school or teacher. So, when anyone felt the need for action, I believe that they contacted one or more of the other special interest groups to get things started. In this affluent setting, I believe there is more likelihood of having this type of relationship than in poorer, less active or less aggressive communities.

Some brief examples of cases involving politics are:

1. The teacher in Chapter II who refused to sign her evaluation or agree to any negative observations was recommended for a transfer by the principal. The transfer request was refused, probably because

her spouse was a well known employee of one of
the state department offices.

2. A principal had a number of teacher vacancies at
the beginning of the year but had sent in recommendations for all but one of them. One of the
local board of education members knew someone
whom she wanted for that position and got the mes-
sage to the personnel office who notified the principal that he was expected to interview and hire
the special candidate. The principal refused, indicating that he would recommend whomever he felt
met the qualifications appropriate for the class. The
personnel office responded that if he did not hire
that person, his other recommendations would not
be approved.

3. An administrator had an assignment that he felt
had grown to the point where he needed an assistant. He requested the additional position in the
budget and two years later a new position was
added. The administrator was not aware of the addition until he saw it advertised on the bulletin
board. The shocking part about the case was that
the administrator had not been told about it and
did not know that the new person was to be his

boss, not his assistant. Because it turned out that not one single qualified applicant applied, a top level administrator was sent to hire a principal whom, I believe, the central office wanted to replace anyway. The worst part of the deal was that the administrator who was in the job was expected to train the ex-principal to be his boss.

4. The saddest situation I have witnessed was the denial of tenure to three black principals. Each of them had completed three years service in good standing, but when the time came to grant them tenure, all three were turned down and demoted to assistant principal. To add insult to injury, a top level administrator, to cover his actions, requested that one of the principals write him a letter requesting the change to the position of assistant principal.

While there might have been some reasons for the way each of the above was handled, I find it difficult to understand why anyone wants to take advantage of anyone or any situation.

There might be reasons other than elections to use politics, but education is certainly not one of them. If we are to do our best for the children, all of our energy is needed to properly teach the children. Nothing less than our best effort given to our jobs should be accepted. Using politics is the selfish way of manipulating or using power to reach an undeserved goal.

HODN

CHAPTER VIII

Some Effects of Integration and Segregation on Education

It is extremely difficult for me to articulate my true feelings about segregation and integration as they are practiced in the country and in our schools. Let me say first that I am definitely against segregation in any form, at any time, in any place, for any reason. My dictionary (The Reader's Digest Great Encyclopedia Dictionary, Second Printing: 1967), defines "integration" as "the act or operation of integrating; the bringing or fitting together of parts into a whole" and "segregation" as "the act or process of segregating (to place apart from others or the rest; isolate)". As I have worked with all levels of school staff, boards of education and parents, I believe that we have done only the bare minimum in the area of integration while holding on to aspects of segregation, in subtle and underhanded ways. It seems as if we have done, for the most part, only what the law, with its many loopholes, has required, and what the voters would be likely to approve if they had the choice.

As I think about integration and segregation in the schools, I naturally compare today's conditions with those when I was young, between about 1933 to the mid-40s. A few of the things come to mind:

1. There was no transportation for black children, some of whom had to walk as much as 2 to 3 miles or more one way.

2. Schools were one-room buildings, in some cases housing grades 1-7. These buildings were located near a community church but, of course, were not a part of it.

3. The children themselves had to keep the building clean and fires going in the pot-bellied stove in order to heat the school.

4. Water had to be drawn from a well, and the bathroom was an outhouse.

5. The only equipment or materials I remember being available were old books and chalk for the chalkboard.

6. Neighboring churches had to be used for any group meetings or special programs.

7. My high school building was an old wood frame building in general disrepair with holes in the floor and dragging doors.
8. The first flushing toilets were installed in 1943-44.
9. No black children were permitted to attend white schools.
10. There was no interaction between black and white schools.

These 10 items hardly begin to give a complete story of the conditions for blacks, not to mention the implications for their education.

Other conditions that didn't reflect directly on education include:

1. Separate water fountains for blacks and whites in public buildings.
2. Blacks being required to use only bathrooms labeled "colored."
3. Blacks being forced to go to the back door of restaurants to be served.
4. In stores, whites being served before blacks.
5. Black men being called "boy" or "uncle."
6. One black person often working while several white "supervisors" stood around doing nothing.
7. Blacks being forced to ride in the back of a bus.

8. Blacks being assaulted by whites who never or rarely got punished.

9. Living in an area where lynching and shootings took place within a 10-mile radius.

10. Blacks being forced to call white females "Miss" after they reached the age of 16.

Unfortunately, I witnessed or experienced all of these practices. While they do not affect education directly, just being aware of these terrible situations could affect black students' classroom behavior.

As I think back through my experiences, I can recall many actions taken by teachers or other staff members that can be classified as being prejudiced or racist. I can not say what motivated them and I'm not sure that the teachers fully realized what they were doing. But even if these actions toward blacks were not intended to be negative or degrading, they were perceived as such by the pupils and other blacks. Among the actions to which I'm referring are:

1. Refusing to welcome children into the classroom in the proper manner. The attitude and actions of the teacher must be welcoming.

2. Refusing to make the pupil feel comfortable in the class.

3. Showing favoritism towards whites in working with

children. Blacks want to be a part of activities as well as whites.

4. Refusal to require a single standard of behavior instead of letting blacks "get away" with things and then blame them. (Mentioned in Chapter VII).

5. Refusal to spend those few extra minutes with the children rather than automatically recommending them for placement in emotionally and behaviorally handicapped classes to get rid of them. (Mentioned in Chapter VII).

6. Refusal to recommend qualified black children for advanced programs.

7. Using abusive, embarrassing or threatening language toward a black child in front of the class.

8. Not involving parents until the point-of-no-return has been reached. (Mentioned in Chapter VII).

9. Stereotyping by comparing test results of blacks and whites.

10. Refusal to use everything they know to teach the black child. Let's use that knowledge!

When I was in the U. S. Navy about 1953, my ship had to go into the Portsmouth, Virginia naval shipyard for repairs. I remember passing bathrooms one day, which had signs above the doors, saying, "Colored" and "White." The next day both signs were gone. I see integration of the schools as being just that simple to implement if we truly want to do it. The attitude and desire are prerequisites. We are way past the point when true integration should have taken place.

Sometimes it appears that segregation is still institutionalized and nationalized. Some time ago, I was watching a syndicated morning live TV show on a day when the host had a black co-host. As they traded information, the host told his co-host that he was the only black guy he knew who was not a good athlete. How sad!

I wish to bring my comments to a close on a positive note. Even though I am definitely against the act of segregating, I do not hold negative feelings toward all white people. In fact, I owe huge debts of gratitude to one white family and one white organization in Danville, Virginia, and another family in Raleigh, North Carolina for the help they gave me in getting to and through college. I will be forever grateful to them for being almost like family to me. It is my hope that examples of this nature exist throughout the country.

CHAPTER IX

Busing

During the 1944-45 school year, I was a student bus driver transporting high school students who lived outside of the walking distance to and from the only high school for blacks in the county. All of these pupils attended regular classes with hope of graduating and fulfilling their goals for life.

Since there were no special education classes, either for gifted children or for those with special needs, buses were used for transporting only pupils in regular classes who lived a certain distance from the school. Schools were not integrated at that time so routes were not complicated or confusing, even though some were lengthy.

As I looked at the use of buses prior to my retirement, I could not really compare their use in '44-'45 with their use in '87-'88. As of today, busing seems to have increased tremendously. Some of the reasons for the changes are:

1. Growing school population,
2. Development of new suburban areas,
3. Addition of new programs,
4. Building of more schools,
5. Changes in philosophy of education and use of buses,
6. Integration, and
7. Developing of specialized magnet schools.

I'm sure that the current staff of any school can provide many more reasons than those identified on my short list.

Every school system has its own reasons and philosophies for busing. I have not seen any system or school that doesn't transport average and handicapped children to their regular school assignments. However, there are districts or systems that have added some specialized programs only in certain schools, requiring additional transportation service. Examples of increased busing are also the result of the many varieties of magnet schools now in existence in many parts of the country. Without this additional transportation, these programs would suffer or be eliminated.

There are some areas of school programming for which extra buses are used that I believe are not providing the results that are generally expected, desirable or fair to the total school community. The two main areas are:

1. Integration (see Chapter VIII): I strongly feel that busing mainly goes in one direction: from black neighborhoods to white neighborhoods. Black parents and pupils are, therefore, left without a "home" school. Receiving schools are ill-prepared to accommodate the black students. The black pupils often do not feel welcome in the new school, resulting in a decline in academic performance and behavior. The group that gets the advantage is the one that refuses to be bused.

2. Magnet Schools (see Chapter III): It is my judgment that the transportation needs of magnet schools serve only a small percentage of the school population and are far more extensive than busing to regular schools. Meeting the needs of magnet schools is unfair to other schools.

I strongly believe that school districts would save money used for these buses and improve the instructional level of black children by returning them to neighborhood schools, at least on the K-5 or K-8 levels—but with teachers of the same quality as are in more affluent schools. Along with this change, I think that programs in every school need to be enriched, not just in the magnet schools. Where would we get the money? It seems to me that buses for transferring pupils for purposes of integrating the schools could be eliminated and the money distributed to improve education.

For this project, I would hope that we can stop thinking politically and do what works, what is practical and what is right. I am positive it will work.